ISBN 978-1-5279-6015-2
PIBN 10932142

1 MONTH OF
FREE
READING

at

www.ForgottenBooks.com

By purchasing this book you are eligible for one month membership to ForgottenBooks.com, giving you unlimited access to our entire collection of over 1,000,000 titles via our web site and mobile apps.

To claim your free month visit:

www.forgottenbooks.com/free932142

English
Français
Deutsche
Italiano
Español
Português

www.forgottenbooks.com

Mythology Photography **Fiction**
Fishing Christianity **Art** Cooking
Essays Buddhism Freemasonry
Medicine **Biology** Music **Ancient
Egypt** Evolution Carpentry Physics
Dance Geology **Mathematics** Fitness
Shakespeare **Folklore** Yoga Marketing
Confidence Immortality Biographies
Poetry **Psychology** Witchcraft
Electronics Chemistry History **Law**
Accounting **Philosophy** Anthropology
Alchemy Drama Quantum Mechanics
Atheism Sexual Health **Ancient History**
Entrepreneurship Languages Sport
Paleontology Needlework Islam
Metaphysics Investment Archaeology
Parenting Statistics Criminology
Motivational

S. Hrg. 109–422

PROPOSED FISCAL YEAR 2007 BUDGET REQUEST FOR THE NATIONAL PARK SERVICE

HEARING

BEFORE THE

SUBCOMMITTEE ON NATIONAL PARKS

OF THE

COMMITTEE ON ENERGY AND NATURAL RESOURCES UNITED STATES SENATE

ONE HUNDRED NINTH CONGRESS

SECOND SESSION

TO

REVIEW THE PRESIDENT'S PROPOSED BUDGET FOR THE NATIONAL PARK SERVICE FOR FISCAL YEAR 2007

MARCH 14, 2006

Printed for the use of the
Committee on Energy and Natural Resources

U.S. GOVERNMENT PRINTING OFFICE

28–080 PDF   WASHINGTON : 2006

For sale by the Superintendent of Documents, U.S. Government Printing Office
Internet: bookstore.gpo.gov Phone: toll free (866) 512–1800; DC area (202) 512–1800
Fax: (202) 512–2250 Mail: Stop SSOP, Washington, DC 20402–0001

PROPOSED FISCAL YEAR 2007 BUDGET REQUEST FOR THE NATIONAL PARK SERVICE

TUESDAY, MARCH 14, 2006

U.S. SENATE,
SUBCOMMITTEE ON NATIONAL PARKS,
COMMITTEE ON ENERGY AND NATURAL RESOURCES,
Washington, DC.

The subcommittee met, pursuant to notice, at 2:30 p.m., in room SD–366, Dirksen Senate Office Building, Hon. Craig Thomas presiding.

OPENING STATEMENT OF HON. CRAIG THOMAS, U.S. SENATOR FROM WYOMING

Senator THOMAS. The time has arrived. We will go ahead and start. Some are not here yet. Starting on time in the Senate is usually lonely. But we are going to have some votes at 3 o'clock, so I think it is important that we get started and we will see who is able to come.

I want to welcome our panel. Certainly, the Honorable Fran Mainella, Director of the Park Service, I am glad to have you here. And Mr. Sheaffer, Comptroller, and Steve Martin, Deputy Director, thank you so much for being here.

Our purpose for the hearing is to receive testimony on the President's proposed budget for the National Park Service for fiscal year 2007. In addition of two new units in February of this year, the National Park Service is responsible for 390 units in 49 States and U.S. territories. Over 23,000 employees support a mission that brings over 270 million visitors to our parks each year.

Beginning in 2001, the budget for the National Park Service gradually increased from $2.2 billion to $2.6 billion in 2004. Then it began to decline in 2005. The President's request for 2007 is $2.16 billion. This is a 5-percent or a $100 million reduction from the 2006 appropriation.

The majority of cuts, I understand, are in construction and I am concerned about the impact this may have on the operation and the maintenance of our parks and ultimately the visitor experience. Heritage areas, studies of new park units, major maintenance, and escalating fixed costs contribute, of course, to the funding challenges of the parks and the services that they must deal with.

I realize, however, that for all of us there needs to be some belt tightening to address the Federal deficit. We need to make sure, however, that any cuts are carefully reviewed and that we can avoid impacting the visitor experience or damaging the resource through neglect. And that is why we are here today.

(1)

So I want to thank you very much for being here. And, as I said, I think really the thrust of why we are here is to get your views of what the budget means, where the changes that may have to be made will be made, and how in your view that will impact services and the resources of the parks. So thank you very much and please go right ahead with your testimony.

[The prepared statements of Senators Menendez and Salazar follow:]

PREPARED STATEMENT OF HON. ROBERT MENENDEZ, U.S. SENATOR FROM NEW JERSEY

Thank you, Mr. Chairman, for providing us the chance to discuss the budget for this very important agency of the Department of Interior, and thank you, Director Mainella, for coming to share your expertise with this committee.

I'm very concerned about the contradictions inherent in this budget proposal. There was an almost $85 million cut for the operations and maintenance of the parks in the budget, along with a $93 million decrease in construction funding. Yet the administration insists that it is living up to the President's campaign promise to help our national parks by ending their decade-long maintenance backlog. To me, this makes no sense. To make matters worse, the National Parks Service (NPS) is pushing a revision of the 2001 Management Policies that is at best unnecessary and at worst a sharp deviation from the principles that caused President Franklin D. Roosevelt to proclaim that "there is nothing so American as our national parks."

The proposed change to the Management Policies threatens to shift the entire focus of the NPS from an agency designed to protect our parks to one designed to get the maximum use out of them. While I wholeheartedly believe that Americans should be able to enjoy their national parks through a wide variety of recreational activities, if we don't put the priority on conservation and protection, there will nothing left for us to enjoy. This shift echoes other Interior policies of late, suc the decrease in the federal Land and Water Conservation Fund program and ing out òf stateside grant program, the expansion of oil rigs along our conti .cal shelf, and the attempted opening of public lands out west for oil and gas ᶜ .ing. Time and time again, the administration's approach to our public lands is ᵗ ᵗry to exploit them for maximum gain, and I fear that this revision to the Mar ᵧement Policies is leading us down that road with our national parks.

Furthermore, in spite of this administration's insistence that their ne   policies are for the benefit of park managers across the country, this revision v .s written and published without their knowledge or input. The process itself rejeᶜ d the very managers and park professionals the document claims as its benefici ies. Such a top-down, politically motivated process is further proof of the super' ᵤity of these rewrites. This rewrite opens the door for increased commercializati ᶇ of the park system, more flight paths across park boundaries, a relaxing of the ᵀ .mits on industrialization in surrounding communities, and a corresponding increᶜ .se in noise and air pollution over the blue skies of our national parks.

I'm also concerned about the delays that have been holding up proposed restoration and rehabilitation projects on Ellis Island, unquestionably one of our nation's most important historic sites. For several years, a dedicated group of private citizens have been working to preserve and protect the portion of Ellis Island that belongs to New Jersey, which although not as well known as the main building, contains structures that are just as historic, and were just as vital for the millions of immigrants who passed through the island seeking a better life in this country. However, their efforts have been delayed by the National Park Service, and I have submitted a question for the record to try to find out why this process is taking so long. I hope we can move forward on Ellis Island quickly to ensure that we don't lose any of its historic structures forever.

In closing, our parks have been a source of national pride for over 100 years, and the implications of this budget proposal, when combined with the proposed changes in the National Parks Service's Management Policies, leave me wondering what types of spaces future generations will be left to enjoy in another 100 years. Will my grandchildren be spending summer days at Sandy Hook, camping in Stokes State Forest, hiking in the Delaware Water Gap, and picnicking in local parks across the state? Or will these spaces be destroyed by rampant development and a federal policy that didn't adequately value conservation? I look forward to working with my colleagues to ensure the continued existence and vibrancy of our parks and open spaces, and I once again thank Director Mainella for being here. Thank you, Mr. Chairman.

Thank you, Mr. Chairman and Ranking Member Akaka. I want to welcome Director Mainella.

The National Park Service manages some of Colorado's most treasured lands and sites, including its four National Parks: Rocky Mountain, Great Sand Dunes, Black Canyon of the Gunnison, and Mesa Verde. I deeply appreciate the work that the Park rangers, the Park Police, the superintendents, and all the National Park Service employees do, day in and day out, to protect these crown jewels. You should be proud that visitor satisfaction at the Parks is over 95%.

There are several aspects of the President's FY2007 budget for the Park Service that are positive. As a former Attorney General for Colorado, I appreciate the additional attention to law enforcement and park safety. Our National Parks should never be sanctuaries for criminals or drugs; we need the right investments in training and personnel to uphold the law and guarantee visitor safety across our expansive parks.

On the whole, however, this year's budget for the National Park Service falls short in helping us meet the challenges that face our park system.

Growing demands on Park resources are placing unprecedented stresses on the resources and infrastructure at our Parks. Years of neglect and underfunding have left the park system with a massive maintenance backlog that this budget does not even begin to address. In fact, this budget cuts construction and maintenance funding by 27%. The maintenance backlog that this Administration promised to eliminate will continue to grow under this budget.

I am also concerned about tax dollars being wasted in the Department of the Interior's attempt to rewrite the Park Service's management policies. These policies were revised just five years ago, after a lengthy and substantive public comment process. I have yet to hear a good explanation for why these policies must be revisited now, given all the other pressures on the agency's budget.

Perhaps the most troubling aspect of this budget is the elimination of the Land and Water Conservation Fund stateside grants program. By the Park Service's own standards, this is one of our most efficient, cost-effective partnerships between the federal government and state and local entities. Since its creation in 1964, it has provided Americans with over 40,000 parks, trails, and open spaces in 94% of our counties.

The LWCF stateside grants program is of particular interest to Colorado's rural counties, many of which could not otherwise afford to build a playground at the elementary school, a walking path near the senior center, or a basketball court for its young people. Congress should restore its commitment to helping Americans be active and stay healthy by making permanent the funding for the LWCF stateside grants program.

I look forward to discussing these issues today with Director Mainella and I thank her for being here.

Thank you, Mr. Chairman.

STATEMENT OF FRAN P. MAINELLA, DIRECTOR, NATIONAL PARK SERVICE, DEPARTMENT OF THE INTERIOR; ACCOMPANIED BY BRUCE SHEAFFER, COMPTROLLER; AND STEVE MARTIN, DEPUTY DIRECTOR

Ms. MAINELLA. Thank you, Mr. Chairman. Again, thank you for holding this hearing on our fiscal year 2007 budget request for the National Park Service. I also want to thank you for your continued support of the work we do in our national parks. You have been a great champion. I also would like to ask that my prepared testimony be included for the record.

Senator THOMAS. It will be included.

Ms. MAINELLA. Thank you, sir. The National Park Service has attained a 96 percent satisfaction level by our park visitors. In 2004 visitation increased by nearly 4 percent, bringing it to nearly 280 million visitors.

In addition, our volunteerism is also up by nearly 14 percent. We have basically 137,000 people volunteering in our parks contributing a record five million hours. Our national parks also provide an annual economic benefit of nearly $12 billion, and have created nearly 250,000 jobs. And as you have indicated we do have 390 units in the system at this time.

This year's budget request of over $2.15 billion for the National Park Service will assist the administration in meeting its goal of cutting the Federal budget deficit in half by 2009. While total proposed funding is $100.5 million below the enacted level for fiscal year 2006, park operating funding would increase by over $23 million. There are a number of key programs that would also be increased and we are grateful for that.

While there will always be challenges, as with any agency or organization, the innovative management approaches and the business practices we are implementing and the dedication and creativity of the 20,000 NPS employees will help us make more effective use of the funding we receive.

The areas of focus include, first of all, visitor services and safety. Of approximately $1.7 billion proposed for the park operations, nearly $1.2 billion is requested for park base funding, a $20.6 million increase over fiscal year 2006.

The fiscal year 2007 request also proposes key investments in visitor health and safety and law enforcement programs, including $500,000 to enhance the investigative capabilities of three of our park regions; $2.8 million for high priority police operations, particularly the U.S. Park Police; and $441,000 for NPS public health programs, including the avian flu issues. Also $750,000 to fund the FLETC training program so that parks will not have to pay for law enforcement training out of their everyday operational budgets.

The second area we focus on, of course, is natural resources and its stewardship. The 2007 budget has $1 million additional for completing the inventory by the 32 networks throughout the National Park System that are identifying the vital signs of 272 natural resource parks. Also, for one of our favorite topics, exotic plants, there is $750,000 in additional money for enhancing our exotic plant management efforts.

The third area is cultural resource stewardship. The fiscal year 2007 budget, if passed, would provide $1 million for our work on cultural landscapes and historic structures. And it includes almost $72 million for Historic Preservation Fund matching grants and Save America's Treasures, Preserve America, and Heritage Partnership programs, which you have been helping with through the heritage areas program legislation.

The fourth area is enhancing the NPS asset management program. This request includes over $393 million for facility maintenance, including a $10 million increase for preventive/cyclic maintenance and $229 million for construction. Included, also, is the $210 million for park roads provided through the Department of Transportation and their budget, and $100 million for maintenance from visitor fees. With this request, the administration will have committed $5.6 billion total to the maintenance backlog during the years 2002 to 2007.

The fifth area of focus is continuing management reforms. One of the ways we are continuing to promote management excellence this year is through the revision of our 2001 Management Policies. As you know this topic has been a subject of a hearing by this committee.

In addition, we are implementing a core operations analysis which will assist park management in making effective decisions on staffing and funding alternatives that tie to core mission goals and ensure funds are spent efficiently. Also, our park scorecard will be included in the regional and servicewide budget formulation process this year.

Two areas which the committee has made suggestions about before are included in the budget. One is for our partnership construction process oversight. The budget includes $310,000 for that. Also, in concessions, which I know is an issue that has come before this committee, $911,000 is for improving our concession oversight.

I know my time has come to an end, Mr. Chairman. I am proud to have great employees and a great leadership team that will assist me in implementing these important strategies as we approach the 100th anniversary of the National Park Service in 2016. We would be very proud to answer any questions that you might have. Thank you, sir.

[The prepared statement of Ms. Mainella follows:]

PREPARED STATEMENT OF FRAN P. MAINELLA, DIRECTOR, NATIONAL PARK SERVICE, DEPARTMENT OF THE INTERIOR

Mr. Chairman and members of the subcommittee, I appreciate the opportunity to appear before you today at this oversight hearing on the FY 2007 budget proposal for the National Park Service (NPS). We thank you for your continuing support of the work we do on behalf of the American people to conserve our Nation's natural and cultural resources and to make them accessible to the public.

The FY 2007 budget request of $2.156 billion for NPS supports goals to protect park resources, continue improvements in asset management, and achieve efficiencies in the management of park programs within the context of the Administration's goal of cutting the Federal budget deficit in half by 2009. Total funding is $100.5 million below the enacted FY 2006 level. However, park operations funding would increase by $23.4 million to $1.742 million. Specific increases for particular programs would strengthen the NPS in a number of key areas, and the innovative management approaches and business practices we are implementing will help us make more effective use of the funding NPS receives.

The FY 2007 budget request also contributes to the NPS Legacy Goals, which are: *management excellence, sustainability, conservation, outdoor recreation, and 21st Century relevancy.* Each goal includes a number of specific objectives, many of which dovetail with the priorities of this budget request. For example, the objectives of our management excellence goal include, among other things, effective law enforcement, improving training programs, continuing partnerships to meet science and research needs, and addressing the concessions backlog. Those are all activities that would be enhanced under this request.

VISITOR SERVICES AND SAFETY

Of the approximately $1.7 billion proposed for park operations, nearly $1.093 billion is requested for "park base" funding, a $20.6 million increase over FY 2006 that will help parks cover most of the cost of increased Federal pay due in FY 2007. The majority of park base funding is provided directly to park managers to pay for operating the parks, including providing for interpretive ranger programs, staffing at visitor centers, daily maintenance activities, and other programs and activities that enhance visitor services and protect resources.

This request sustains and builds on the significant park base increases of the two previous fiscal years—$25 million in FY 2006 and $63 million in FY 2005—that NPS received due to Congress's strong support for the National Park System. Enactment of the FY 2007 request will result in park base funding rising by $177 million, or 19 percent, since FY 2001. The FY 2007 request proposes key investments in visitor health and safety and law enforcement programs, including:

- $500,000 for placing special agents in parks. These park-based special agents would provide investigative support for ranger staffs in parks that extend over large geographic areas, have numerous access points, and are in areas of Federal jurisdiction where State and local agencies many not have the authority, funding, or personnel to perform these services.
- $750,000 for base funding for the Federal Law Enforcement Training Center (FLETC). Centrally funding FLETC, instead of paying for law enforcement training from individual park budgets, will allow parks to dedicate critical law enforcement funds to on-the-ground visitor and resource protection while still ensuring that essential training is made available to law enforcement personnel.
- $2.8 million for high priority police operations, including icon park security and recruitment and training for the U.S. Park Police (USPP). This is expected to increase the force to 620 sworn officers by the end of FY 2007, up from 603 at the start of FY 2006. A comprehensive review of USPP Force requirements was conducted in accordance with recommendations contained in the recent National Academy of Public Administration (NAPA) report. This funding would ultimately achieve a force strength recommended as a result of the review that followed the NAPA report.
- $441,000 for the NPS Public Health Program, allowing NPS to adequately respond to potential outbreaks and disease transmission issues, and to conduct routine evaluations for safety of food, drinking water, wastewater, and vectorborne disease risks in parks. The request also sustains $525,000 received in FY 2006 supplemental funding to address avian influenza.

NATURAL RESOURCES STEWARDSHIP

The FY 2007 request includes some specific increases to help address some of our most pressing natural resource protection needs, including:

- $2.4 million for funding NPS' commitments under the National Parks Air Tour Management Act of 2000, which directs the NPS and the Federal Aviation Administration to collaborate on developing commercial air tour management plans for all parks where this activity occurs. These plans will help managers prevent or minimize adverse impacts on natural soundscapes and visitor experiences.
- $1 million for completing a system of 32 networks throughout the National Park System that are identifying the "vital signs" of 272 natural resource parks. These inventory and monitoring networks share fieldwork, staff, equipment, and business practices leading to successful new partnerships with universities and researchers through Cooperative Ecosystem Studies Units and Research Learning Centers.
- $750,000 for enhancing existing exotic plant management teams to address severe damage caused by invasive species to natural resources and the economy. These teams will operate in three priority geo-regional areas—South Florida, the Northern Great Plains, and the Rio Grande River Basin.

CULTURAL RESOURCES STEWARDSHIP

As part of the Administration's Preserve America initiative, the FY 2007 budget request proposes to focus resources for Preserve America grants, Save America's Treasures grants, and the Heritage Partnership program into a unified $32.2 million American Heritage and Preservation Partnership. This initiative would allow for better coordination and greater efficiencies in meeting the Administration's goals for enhancing and expanding opportunities for cultural resource preservation. The combining of these programs would allow local communities to determine which strategies best suit their heritage needs and to apply to the most appropriate programs to conserve heritage resources and promote heritage tourism. Other cultural resource investments in the FY 2007 request include:

- $1 million to initiate an effort to provide complete, accurate, and reliable information about cultural landscapes and historic and prehistoric structures, enabling NPS to make significant progress toward updating the Cultural Landscapes Inventory and the List of Classified Structures (Historic and Prehistoric) in FY 2007.
- $39.7 million for Historic Preservation Fund matching grants to States, Territories, and Tribes to preserve historically and culturally significant sites.

ENHANCING THE NPS ASSET MANAGEMENT PROGRAM

The FY 2007 request continues the Administration's substantial investment in reducing the NPS deferred maintenance backlog. The request includes $393.5 million for facility maintenance, including a $10 million increase for cyclic maintenance, and $229.3 million for construction. Including the $210 million for p   roads provided through the Department of Transportation and $100 million foanlnaintenance from visitor fees, the Administration's deferred maintenance investment from FY 2002-FY 2007 would total $5.6 billion. Despite a reduction in line-item construction of $93 million, the $933 million effort in FY 2007 toward reducing the deferred maintenance backlog is exactly equal to the five-year average effort from FY 2002-FY 2006. These investments have enabled NPS to make significant improvements in the condition of critical facilities and other assets that serve visitors and protect park resources.

In addition, NPS is transforming the agency's approach to managing and addressing its deferred maintenance backlog. During the past four years, NPS has been implementing the initial phase of an innovative asset management program focused on developing, for the first time, a comprehensive inventory and condition assessment of the agency's asset base, which includes everything from nearly 18,000 buildings to approximately 15,000 miles of paved and unpaved roads. Condition assessments on eight industry-standard assets, such as buildings, water systems, roads, and trails, will be completed at all parks by the end of 2006. Parks also have completed, for the first time, a prioritization of their asset inventory. This shift in emphasis for the agency is based on management reforms and performance measures, and features a state-of-the-art software system. These new tools will allow NPS to have a better understanding of the true cost of owning and operating structures. NPS also will be able to refine budget estimates and identify maintenance needs based on the actual condition of facilities, and identify the resources needed to bring the highest priority assets to an acceptable condition. Because of NPS's new approach to managing deferred maintenance, managers have a better understanding of both the quantity and condition of park assets, and greater accuracy when discussing park needs and accomplishments.

CONTINUING MANAGEMENT REFORM

The NPS is being innovative and working toward reform in the way it manages natural and cultural resources, as well as in the way it manages money and information.

One of the ways we are continuing to promote management excellence this year is through the revision of the 2001 management policies. In response to the request of the House Subcommittee on National Parks, the NPS has begun the process of updating the policies—which is our guidebook for park managers to implement the NPS Organic Act—to ensure that we conserve the resources unimpaired for the enjoyment of future generations, while providing for their current enjoyment. After an extensive public comment period which ended on February 25, the next step is for the comments to be compiled, considered, and reviewed by our career leadership team. The edited document will then be submitted to NPS employees and the National Park Service Advisory Board before any final product is approved by NPS and the Department. The proposed revisions would provide greater flexibility and tools for superintendents to make better and more informed decisions. They would maintain our strong commitment to the fundamental mission of the NPS to protect and allow for appropriate enjoyment of parks. One of the primary guiding principles is that, when there is conflict between the protection of resources and their use, conservation will be predominant.

In an attempt to move toward greater levels of budget and performance accountability, the NPS continues to expand the use of the Program Assessment Rating Tool (PART), activity-based costing, and preliminary planning efforts associated with competitive reviews. PART evaluations and recommendations continue to inform both budget formulation and program management decisions. PART reviews were conducted on four NPS program areas for the FY 2007 Budget Request: Visitor Services, External Programs—Technical Assistance, External Programs—Financial Assistance, and Concessions Management. The NPS has completed ten PART reviews since FY 2002 and is planning one PART review for the FY 2008 budget cycle.

The NPS continually works to further the integration of budget and performance. Over the past year, efforts have focused on a new core operations analysis process and the development of a NPS Park Scorecard. Our Core Operations Analysis is designed to assist park management in making fully informed decisions on staffing and funding alternatives that are based on realistic funding projections and tie to core mission goals. This process will ensure that funds are spent in support of a park's purpose, that funds are spent in an efficient manner, that a park's request for funding is based on accurate data, and that there are adequate funds and staff to preserve and protect the resources for which parks are responsible. The NPS goal is to integrate management tools, such as the Budget Cost Projection Model, Business Plans, Core Operations Analysis, and the Park Scorecard, to provide a more qualitative basis for decision-making.

The Park Scorecard is designed to be an indicator of park financial, operational, and managerial performance. It is used, in conjunction with other factors, to identify and evaluate base budget increases and potential park performance if budget increases are received. The scorecard is used together with the Operations Formulation System (OFS) to offer context for proposed base budget increases and will eventually be integrated within the OFS system. In 2006, the newest version of the Park Scorecard will be tested, piloted, and integrated into the Regional and Servicewide budget formulation processes leading to a national priority list for park base funding requests for use in future budgets.

Two proposed increases in the FY 2007 request that would contribute significantly to improved management are:

- $310,000 for managing and supporting the newly established Partnership Construction Process (Building Better Partnerships Program). The Service would secure outside expertise to assess the capacity of partners to raise funds and evaluate business models for economic development. The increase would also be used to manage the Monitoring and Tracking Database System to monitor fundraising efforts and partner construction projects, generate reports, and maintain the partnership webpage.
- $911,000 for improving concessions contracting oversight so NPS can achieve its program goals of reducing the contracting backlog and effectively managing the concessions program.

OTHER PROGRAMS

As part of the President's effort to cut the budget deficit in half by 2009, the Administration had to make difficult choices in its FY 2007 budget request that resulted in reduced funding for some lower-priority programs. Funding for LWCF State grants is not being requested, with the exception of $1.6 million to administer prior year grants. However, the request continues a limited amount of funding for Federal land acquisition, of which nearly $22.7 million would be for the NPS portion of the Federal land acquisition program, including $5 million to acquire critical land at the Flight 93 National Memorial and $4 million to continue the Civil War Battlefield Preservation Grants program. These Civil War grants would garner a minimum of $4 million in matching funds.

Mr. Chairman, that concludes my summary of the FY 2007 budget request for NPS. We would be pleased to answer any questions you and the other members of the subcommittee may have.

Senator THOMAS. Well, thank you.

Ms. MAINELLA. I tried to zip through that.

Senator THOMAS. Good job.

Ms. MAINELLA. Thank you.

[Laughter.]

Senator THOMAS. I am going to get over there to vote after all. Well, that is great. And I think you touched on many of the items that are there.

It is my understanding, then, that this $100 million less, which represents 5 percent of your funding, much of that will come out of either construction or maintenance. Is that correct?

Ms. MAINELLA. It is from construction, land acquisition, and a program that I know many of us certainly have enjoyed, the land and water conservation fund State grants.

Senator THOMAS. I see. How does construction tie in or what is the relationship between that and backlog management?

Ms. MAINELLA. Well, in this budget there is $933 million worth of maintenance backlog funding. So we continue to move forward on that. As you know, construction does address not only new facilities, but sometimes rehabilitation of facilities that were in difficult condition. We do feel, though, that we are taking major steps forward on the maintenance backlog. And, if you remember, the President made a commitment of $4.9 billion that would be used to address the backlog. With this budget, we will be at $5.6 billion in that effort.

Senator THOMAS. The question of backlog has been there for some time of course and you have been making some progress. What will this do, in your view and generally, to the growth or to the percentage of progress that you will be making?

Ms. MAINELLA. Well, I think that, again, we are moving very positively. We will increase in this budget by $10 million the focus on cyclic maintenance, which means that we will have gone from the year 2002, I believe, where we had about $24 million, up to now about $71 million in cyclic, which means we are trying to get in a preventive stage.

Now we did drop the repair/rehab down by $10 million, but we expect that through some of our fees that are coming in that you have helped us with, we will use about 50 percent of those fees toward maintenance. We feel that will help balance or at least be part of that effort.

As far as measuring our maintenance backlog, no longer are we doing that by how much money we spend. We have done 6,000 projects toward maintenance. But we do look at it under what is called a facility condition index. And in the green book there are charts that deal with how each area, each region, is addressing what are called standard assets, their paved roads and structures, and where they plan to be at the end of 2007 as far as that facility condition index goes. It will make some movement forward.

It is still going to be a process; as you know, there is really never an end to the maintenance backlog. There always will be a backlog. We just had hurricanes. I guarantee you, even with the hope that you will all support the supplemental for hurricanes for National Parks, $55.4 million, we will still have damaged facilities in a "backlog" status because it is going to take us a year or more to certainly work on those.

Senator THOMAS. Okay. All right. Thank you. Senator Alexander, we started right on time because we are going to have to end here soon. Would you care to make an opening statement?

Senator ALEXANDER. So she has not yet——

Senator THOMAS. She has.

Senator ALEXANDER. Oh, she has.

Ms. MAINELLA. I zipped on through it. Sorry.

Senator ALEXANDER. I would like to——

Senator THOMAS. She referred to all of your requests in the budget.

[Laughter.]

Senator ALEXANDER. Well, thank you, Mr. Chairman. Would it be appropriate for me to ask a couple of questions?

Senator THOMAS. Absolutely. Go right ahead.

Senator ALEXANDER. Okay. Good. Thank you for being here. And I will make my questions brief. First, I want to thank you for the work you have been doing with our committee, with the chairman and others of us who are interested in the management policies.

Ms. MAINELLA. Thank you.

Senator ALEXANDER. Because all of us are concerned about that. And I look forward to the hearing that, I believe, is planned for later on down the road on that subject.

Ms. MAINELLA. Yes, sir.

Senator ALEXANDER. But in a recent hearing with Secretary Norton, I asked her questions about what would happen when there is a conflict between the protection of resources and use and other needs in the park. And what would be predominate. And I noticed that you say in your testimony today that your reforms would maintain our strong commitment to the fundamental mission of the National Park Service to protect and allow for appropriate enjoyment. One of the primary guiding principles is that when there is a conflict between the protection of resources and their use conservation will be predominate.

Ms. MAINELLA. Yes, sir.

Senator ALEXANDER. And I also received a letter from Secretary Norton today making that clear. So I appreciate very much that statement and hope that is a guiding principle in the management policies that you are developing because I think that will relieve a lot of the concerns that some of us had about the direction some things were going.

Ms. MAINELLA. Senator, again, after our meeting with you we had some discussion with the Secretary and as a result, you do have a letter in front of you that she did send that does reaffirm what both Deputy Steve Martin and I have said in our testimonies dealing with management policies and budget, that when there is a conflict then conservation will be predominate. Obviously we will continue to work together to hopefully, as we do in anything, to just avoid conflicts where possible. But, when there is a conflict we will have conservation as predominate. Yes, sir.

Senator ALEXANDER. Thank you very much. Now on the Landwater Conservation Fund, without—this is a tight budget year. And I understand that. But, as we have discussed before there are two opportunities that might present an opportunity for something like a conservation royalty of the kind Wyoming enjoys on oil on its property. That when we have offshore drilling that we might take some of those resources and devote them to conservation purposes. Something like a conservation royalty to a State. I don't want to take away any other—any existing. I just would like to see more of that. One of those is if we were to pass Landwater, which several of us are for, there is in the budget a reserve fund that would devote some of the revenues, a billion dollars over 3 years, to conservation purposes.

A second is in the discussion of Lease 181. There has been some discussion that there might be a conservation royalty that would go to State Landwater Conservation Fund, which is a popular program, important program, and there is not much controversy about the State Landwater Conservation Program.

I would hope that you and the administration, if those two pieces of legislation make their way through Congress, will fight to keep in the legislation the special funding for the Landwater Conservation Fund.

Ms. MAINELLA. Senator, as a past administrator of the stateside Land and Water Conservation Fund grants, we believe that it is a very important program. We know that in the PART review that OMB has worked with us on there are areas we need to improve upon. But we would be very honored to work along with you, and any other members of this committee or others, to assist in finding a way to assist with the stateside funding. And I do offer Comptroller Bruce Sheaffer to assist in any of his areas of expertise to help you in that effort.

Senator ALEXANDER. Thank you.

Mr. Chairman, is there time for one more question?

Senator THOMAS. Yes, sir.

Senator ALEXANDER. Did you all discuss the funding for salary increases yet today? I wanted to ask you to make sure I understand it. As I understand it, when we do not increase funding enough, and we order you to pay a salary increase, you have to take that funding out of operation funds for the park.

Ms. MAINELLA. Yes, sir.

Senator ALEXANDER. So while it might seem like there is more money for maintenance and there is more money for, well not maintenance, but there is more money for operations of the park, in fact there is less than one might hope because you had to take some of that out to pay salaries. That is going to be true with this budget, is it not? I mean you are going to have to take some money out of operations to pay salaries of park employees. And to what extent is that true and how does that compare with what has happened in past years?

Ms. MAINELLA. Senator, in this particular budget, again, the Secretary and others have really helped us to try to keep as much of the focus on every day park operations as possible. And as a result we do have coming year salaries of a little over a $20 million increase. This will cover about 70 percent of the salary increase as proposed in this budget, which is at a 2.2 percentage level for both civilian and military personnel.

Of course, if the salary increase goes any higher than that 2.2, then we would be absorbing a greater percentage than the 30 percent that is reflected here. I do want to comment though that last year we did come to you with a request for 100 percent of our salaries to be covered. But in the end, because of the difference between military and others, and other things, the way the bottom line is that we still ended up absorbing about 30 percent, because there was, as you know—necessary because of hurricanes—an across-the-board 1 percent cut that was assessed in the 2006 budget. So we are functioning in the 2006 budget with about a 70 percent fixed-cost level covered.

Also, just for your further information, from 1994 until 2004 we were running at about 60 percent coverage of our salaries. So it has been a problem in the past in having that. And when we do have to absorb, again, we have great employees. They find creative ways to do that. But, it does mean that they have to make some managerial decisions.

Senator ALEXANDER. Thank you, Mr. Chairman. It looks like we may need a little truth in legislating provision for ourselves because we are maybe making it look like we are providing more money for the operations of parks when in effect it might be 60 or 70 percent of what it looks like.

I have a couple of other questions. I will just submit them to her to be answered later.

Senator THOMAS. Thank you, sir. I have a couple of more questions, Director. As you might imagine when we talk about reductions, then people ask are there going to be increases in entrance fees and those kinds of things. Is that on anyone's mind?

Ms. MAINELLA. Well, as you know, this committee has helped us to move from a fee demo program to a permanent fee effort. And those fees have been very important in all our parks. And, again, they do not cover everyday operations. They are to cover additional visitor services, and part of that is making sure our facilities are in good shape.

We have gone out through civic engagement, public involvement, to communities to find out views on increasing a fee where our superintendents have made recommendations to us in that regard. And there are going to be determinations, based on working with the communities and working with our superintendents, and the environmental community and others, that it would probably be beneficial to some parks to have some increases. I think we are forecasting approximately 23 units that might be considering increases. That is out of 390. But I think, again, our fee increases may cover up to about $10 million.

Senator THOMAS. So this is sort of the normal increase.

Ms. MAINELLA. Yes, it is normal. And because of the legislation, we are going to be able to look at this on a regular basis. But, again, we always have to make sure our parks are accessible for all economic levels. And we need to make sure, again, that people are comfortable with any fees we move forward with.

Senator THOMAS. So these are not designed to take up reduction?

Ms. MAINELLA. No, no offset at all. It is very important.

Senator THOMAS. What about as we go forward? You have 390 units and there are other things. What impact does this have, as we look in the future and here on this table there will be some more requests for other units to be formed?

Ms. MAINELLA. Mr. Chairman, I think it is really important. Our testimony will still continue to show, I would expect, that we will be very hesitant to ever add on new units in the National Park System, but we will do it when appropriate. There are places that are just exceptional, as we have just seen with the African Burial Ground in New York City where 20,000 enslaved and free Africans died there from the 1600's to the 1700's. When something like that comes to us—and this particular opportunity came to us with moneys to operate it and a visitor center to assist us—we are going to look at those. Also, the Carter G. Woodson Home that is here in Washington, D.C. just came in. It did not come with that aspect, but still, it was so critical, I think, to the story of this country that we have to make those value decisions. And when we do, we do it very cautiously. And we ask that you work with us on that effort.

Senator THOMAS. We will all have to take a little closer look at what the values are. Now, as I recall, you do get highway funds that are outside of this budget. Is that correct?

Ms. MAINELLA. We do get $210 million thanks to the Federal Highways bill that helps us. If you remember, the maintenance backlog, when it was first defined at $4.9 billion, $2.7 billion—more than 50 percent of that—was roads, because that is one of our big issues. And with the Federal Highways Program, I know this is going to help us immensely. So this is outside of our budget.

Senator THOMAS. I am a little parochial. I was up, Steve, in Teton Park last week looking at the roads. But they were all covered up with snow so I could not really——

Mr. MARTIN. We got a lot of snow this year.

Senator THOMAS. Yes, there really was. It was great. Speaking of that, however, being a little parochial, we have had a long-term transportation planning process in Teton Park. What is the status of that, and why is it being delayed as much as it has?

Mr. MARTIN. The plan, I think we are hopefully on its last home stretch here. We had to redo the plan that was first put together by our park, Grand Teton, recently because some of the provisions in it were well beyond what we could reasonably expect to fund. So whereas we still have some of that in there, we had to characterize it in a way that emphasizes things that we feel we can accomplish in the next 10 to 15 years.

And then, also, we wanted to take a closer look at some of the trail provisions and make sure that we had a good viable multi-use trail system that connected with the community, so we sent it back. And we apologize for the delays, but we should be in the home stretch here.

Senator THOMAS. That is good. Maybe we can get more money out from Everglades, do you suppose?

[Laughter.]

Senator THOMAS. You have a question? More? Go right ahead. We will go until the bell rings.

Senator ALEXANDER. Okay. Thanks. First, Mr. Chairman, I would like to ask if I could include in the record the letter from Secretary Norton to me following up our conversation about the predominate purpose of national parks.

Senator THOMAS. It will be in the record.

[The information referred to follows:]

DEPARTMENT OF THE INTERIOR,
Washington, DC, March 14, 2006.

Hon. LAMAR ALEXANDER,
U.S. Senate, Washington, DC.

DEAR SENATOR ALEXANDER: I wanted to follow up on our conversation that occurred during the recent March 2, hearing on the Department of the Interior 2007 budget and to assure you that our disagreement with regard to the draft 2005 Management Policies was more a question of semantics than substance.

I believe that current and future enjoyment of the parks depends upon maintaining unimpaired park resources. That is our statutory obligation. At the hearing, I quoted to you the relevant portion of the 1961 Organic Act that describes the mission of the NPS. That section states:

"[the] purpose is to conserve the scenery and the natural and historic objects and the wildlife therein and to provide for the enjoyment of the same in such manner and by such means as will leave them unimpaired for the enjoyment of future generations."

The quote you cited in the hearing was from the 2001 Management Policies, not the 1916 Organic Act. Management of parks presents complex challenges, since park managers have to address use and impacts consistent with the overarching mission of the parks, which is to protect park resources and values to ensure that these resources and values are maintained unimpaired. This statutory directive inherently required careful evaluation of uses, scientific study, monitoring, and other factors.

Both Director Fran Mainella and Deputy Director Steve Martin, in public statements, including February 2006 testimony presented to the Congress, have stated, and I agree, that when there is a conflict between the protection of resources and use, conservation will be predominant. This recognizes that while we welcome public use and enjoyment in our parks, we will not allow uses that cause unacceptable impact, are inconsistent with park purposes or values, unreasonably interfere with park programs or activities, disrupt the operation of park concessions or contractors, create an unsafe or unhealthful environment for visitors or employees, result in significant conflict with other appropriate uses, or diminish opportunities for current or future generations to enjoy park resources and values. We recognize that the conservation of park natural, cultural, and historic resources provides the foundation for public enjoyment of our national parks.

Parks serve a very important function in our society. They are not wilderness areas, unless specifically designated as such. If "conservation" is viewed as a wilderness standard requiring that all resources remain in their pristine state, we would have no visitor centers, no ranger housing, no hotels, and no roads in parks. While a few of us would be able to enjoy these areas in their pristine state, the classic American family vacation of loading the kids in the care and driving through Yellowstone or the Great Smokies would not exist. Parks fulfill an important visitor service function. They provide education and enjoyment and an introduction to the great outdoors for many who would otherwise miss an inspiring experience.

Over the years, since adoption of the Organic Act, our understanding of caring for parks has evolved. In the past, park managers erroneously allowed eradication of predators, feeding of wild animals, and building of visitor centers in sensitive area that damaged resources. All of these today would be considered inconsistent with the Organic Act and the conservation of the parks. To make proper decisions we need policies that stress sustainable cooperative conservation that works for managing the birthplace of Dr. Martin Luther King as well as managing the bison herd at Yellowstone, not a simple litmus test or bumper sticker phrase that lacks practical efficacy.

The 2005 proposed Management Policies are in draft form. This is why we have put them out for public comment and are now evaluating those comments. I am confident that our policies, when completed by the Director and her career staff, will accomplish this difficult task.

I believe both you and I have the same goals for our national parks. I want Americans to love our national parks, and that love arises when people are encouraged to visit. I want their experiences to be thoroughly enjoyable because they see spectacular scenery, encounter abundant wildlife, and use clean and comfortable facilities. I am confident that our park managers will be able to achieve this in a manner consistent with the Organic Act of 1916.

Please don't hesitate to call me if you would like to talk further about this manner.

Sincerely,

GALE A. NORTON,
Secretary.

Senator ALEXANDER. And second, Madam Director, you and I have talked before about the proposed North Shore road in the Great Smoky Mountain National Park, which has been called for a long time the road to nowhere. At least those who are against it call it that. And the National Park Service is in the final part of an environmental impact statement on that. It is called that by a great many people in North Carolina and Tennessee especially.

If I have it right, the draft environmental impact statement suggested that fully building the road might cost up to $600 million. Even a partial building of the road to the Bushnell area might cost $110 million. Well, the annual road budget for the Great Smoky Mountain Park is only about $9 or $10 million, so the cost of this road would be three times, I believe, the National Park Service's own annual road budget.

What I am getting around to is that all of us have recognized for 40 years that the United States has an obligation to Swain County, North Carolina, as a result of agreements made when the National Park was created. And there was a contract signed by the Tennessee Valley Authority, the State of North Carolina, Swain County, and the Department of the Interior.

The Supreme Court said 40 years ago that in changed circumstances it was not necessary to build a road. I support the idea of a monetary cash settlement to Swain County. So does the State of North Carolina, according to its Governor. So do the elected officials of Swain County.

The third signatory to the agreement was the Tennessee Valley Authority, and I have a letter from Chairman Bill Baxter to Secretary Norton today which says that they agree that the—the TVA agrees that the National Park Service's—with the National Park Service that the alternative with the least environmental impact is the one that does not involve any construction.

So that only leaves the Department of the Interior of the four signatories. Now I know there are different opinions about this, but three of the four signatories have now said that the road is not a good idea. The two U.S. Senators from Tennessee agree with that. The Governor of Tennessee, as well as the Governor of North Carolina agree with that.

I think out of fairness to the people of Swain County we should pull together to try to see if we can come up with a monetary settlement. And I know you do not have a solution to that today, but I think—I would urge you, if you can, to help bring this to a conclusion. It seems to me totally impractical, a waste of tax money, and an environmental disaster to build a $600 million road to the Great Smoky Mountain National Park at this stage. And we are just failing to meet our obligation to the people of Swain County if we do not shift gears and begin to focus on how we can do that through a cash settlement instead.

I would like to include, if I may, Mr. Chairman, this letter from the Chairman of the Tennessee Valley Authority dated March 10.

Senator THOMAS. It will be included.

[The information referred to follows:]

TENNESSEE VALLEY AUTHORITY,
March 10, 2006.

Hon. GALE A. NORTON,
Secretary, Department of the Interior, Washington, DC.

DEAR SECRETARY NORTON: The Tennessee Valley Authority (TVA) is a cooperating agency in the preparation of the Environmental Impact Statement (EIS) on the North Snore Road Project in Swain County, North Carolina. In that capacity, we are currently reviewing the Draft EIS and anticipate submitting comments as a cooperating agency at a later date. TVA is also a party to the 1943 agreement under which construction of the North Shore Road is contemplated. I am writing you today to apprise you of TVA's position on this proposal.

TVA agrees with the National Park Service's (NPS) determination that the alternative with the least environmental impact is the one that does not involve construction; namely, the Monetary Settlement Alternative. Accordingly, we concur in the identification of this alternative as the Environmentally Preferred Alternative for the purposes of *National Environmental Policy Act* review.

The Draft EIS did not identify NPS's preferred alternative to allow consideration of public comments on the completed environmental analyses and revised cost estimates for the build alternatives. These public comments and environmental analyses will also help inform the decisions TVA may have to make about this. Based upon our preliminary review, TVA believes the range of identified alternatives is appropriate and that any of the action alternatives could potentially form the basis for an agreement discharging the Department of Interior from any remaining obligations under the 1943 agreement.

TVA has already fulfilled its obligations under the 1943 agreement by acquiring and transferring to the U.S. Department of Interior approximately 44,000 acres of land on the north shore of Fontana Reservoir. Should the other parties to the 1943 agreement reach consensus on the North Shore Road issue and decide to enter into a new agreement, TVA would be pleased to review the proposal and determine if we should become a party to the new agreement.

Sincerely,

BILL BAXTER,
Chairman.

Ms. MAINELLA. Thank you, Senator. Also, just a comment. Steven Martin is going to, I think for the first time, go to the Great Smokies as he leaves here today. So, he will have a chance to get more familiar with these issues as well. Thank you.

Senator THOMAS. Okay. Thank you.

A proposed budget has placed funding of the National Heritage Areas under the Historic Preservation Fund. What authority do you have to fund National Heritage Areas in this manner?

Ms. MAINELLA. I am going to ask Bruce Sheaffer, if he would, to comment on that for me, please.

Mr. SHEAFFER. We have included appropriation language that would allow it so it would be commensurate with the passage of the bill. We would have the authority if it is passed as now written.

Senator THOMAS. Okay. Will the use of that fund cause a reduction in the funds for the preservation grants or other funds for State historic preservation offices?

Mr. SHEAFFER. Not specifically, no. They would not in any way affect the use of the other funds. No. No, they would not.

Senator THOMAS. Okay.

Mr. SHEAFFER. I gather that the intent of the question is that we are not even requesting the full amount that is made available in the Historic Preservation Fund this year or have not for many years. So, no. It will minimally affect the total amount of the unappropriated balance in the Historic Preservation Fund, if that is the nature of your question.

Senator THOMAS. Yes. Well, there are broader opportunities to use it for other things there. And I am just wondering what impact it would have.

Mr. SHEAFFER. Yes, sir. That is correct.

Senator THOMAS. The administration proposes an offset of a million dollars to cut services by filming permits. Do you anticipate an increase in the revenue from this source?

Ms. MAINELLA. Mr. Chairman, I do believe that we are looking at about a $1.6 million increase as a result. Don Murphy was not able to join us today. He is the deputy that is overseeing those efforts. But there is, if my understanding is correct, action that will be taking place next month to give us the authority to be able to collect these location fees, which we have not been able to actually do thus far. Is that correct, Bruce?

Mr. SHEAFFER. That is correct. We will be operating under an interim plan awaiting final certification of a regulation that would apply to all Federal land-managing agencies. And in the interim we will be applying a rate structure that is the equal to the BLM structure that they have posted. So, yes, we expect additional revenues to offset this decrease.

Senator THOMAS. I see. Good. It would be interesting to note that the budget projects a $6.5 million decrease in fixed costs for interpretation and education of rangers. Fixed costs in this program are declining while fixed costs for other programs are not; why is that?

Ms. MAINELLA. Let me just first of all start this by being very clear. We do not cut our interpretive rangers; they are critical. Their core mission is, as Steve Martin would call it, to the Park Service. What we have is a budget effort that just moves them from one place to another. And I would turn to Bruce to help further explain that in a better way for me.

Mr. SHEAFFER. It is kind of an anomaly of the budget. We propose in this budget to shift the funding for the Harpers Ferry Center from the ONPS account to the construction account. And what you see is the effect of that shift. If that were not part of the formula here, there would actually be a net increase of about $3.8 million on that line you reference.

Senator THOMAS. I see. Okay. Well as strongly as I feel about parks and the preservation, as we all do, in this kind of a budget setting and this sort of a deficit situation, we have to manage a little differently and a little better. So I admire your efforts to take a relatively small reduction and adjust your management in such a way that you can continue to provide the services that are there and protect the resource and do the job that the parks are all about.

So, we have about 1 minute, Mr. Alexander.

Senator ALEXANDER. I can do a 30 second question.

Ms. MAINELLA. But can I do a 30 second answer?

Senator THOMAS. Let's time him and see.

Senator ALEXANDER. Could you tell us how the Park Service is doing to budget operational funding increases for the Chickamauga and Chattanooga National Military Park for staff and interpretive resources? Congress directed funding for the Park Service to begin stabilization of the riverbank in the Moccasin Bend Archeological Area of the Chickamauga Chattanooga National Park last year. And if you do not have that right on your fingertips, you could answer it in a letter.

Ms. MAINELLA. I am looking over to Mr. Sheaffer here quickly. But, again, as you know, both you and Congressman Wamp and others have played an important role in adding Moccasin Bend to our unit, which is an important cultural resource to us. And I know we are trying to do all we can. But I don't know, Bruce, do we have that answer or do we need to get back on that?

Mr. SHEAFFER. Well, for a complete answer we need to get back. We have the status report and they are making progress on it. There will be future budget requests to finish the entire stabilization job up. But they are advancing.

Senator ALEXANDER. I would appreciate a report when you have time. And I know Congressman Wamp would enjoy seeing it as well.

Mr. SHEAFFER. Yes.

Senator ALEXANDER. Thank you.

Mr. SHEAFFER. By all means.

Senator THOMAS. Thank you guys. I am sorry we could not chat a little more. But I do feel comfortable with what you are doing with this budget and certainly we will continue to work with you as time goes by.

Ms. MAINELLA. I just want to thank both of you and other members of the committee that I had a chance to visit with in advance of this hearing. I really appreciate the time you afforded me. Thank you.

Senator THOMAS. Thank you. We appreciate it. We look forward to working with you.

[Whereupon, at 3:05 p.m., the hearing was adjourned.]

APPENDIX

RESPONSES TO ADDITIONAL QUESTIONS

RESPONSES OF FRAN MAINELLA TO QUESTIONS FROM SENATOR THOMAS

Question 1a. Budget Decrease: The Administration's FY 2007 budget for the National Park Service is $100 million less than FY 2006. That represents a 5 percent decrease in funding.

Can we expect to see any reduction in park operations or visitor services as a result of the budget cuts?

Answer. The 2007 budget request maintains the funding levels provided in the 2006 appropriation, which included a net increase of more than $24.6 million over 2005 park base funding. The 2007 budget request is a net increase of $23.4 million above the 2006 enacted level, which includes increases for salaries, benefits, and other fixed costs.

The 2007 budget also proposes key investments in visitor services, health and safety, and law enforcement programs that impact the visitor experience. The budget includes an increase of $250,000 to strengthen the Service's capability to understand opinions about parks by expanding and refining the visitor services survey program. The budget also includes $500,000 for park-based special agents that will provide investigative support to park ranger staffs in parks. In addition, $750,000 is included to centrally fund the Federal Law Enforcement Training Center. An increase of $441,000 is requested to allow NPS to adequately respond to outbreaks and disease transmissions, as well as conduct safety evaluations of park food, drinking water, wastewater and vector-borne disease risks in the parks.

Funding these increases, in conjunction with the combined implementation of ongoing management improvements, will ensure the continuation of enhancements to visitors and other services provided in 2006.

Question 1b. Do you anticipate raising entrance fees or other user fees to overcome budget shortfalls as a result of the proposed cuts in 2007?

Answer. About 14 park units are considering raising entrance fees in 2007 based on a pricing model proposed in 2006 to provide consistency and meet park visitor needs. In addition, some parks are likely to request changes to some expanded amenity fees (user fees) for 2007 based on comparability studies. However, there is no direct link between the prospective fee increases and the proposed budget reductions. The largest part of the $100.5 million reduction in the NPS budget ($84.5 million) is in the Construction account. That reduction will not be offset by fee revenues. NPS plans to use $95 million in fee revenue for maintenance projects in FY 2006 and $100 million in FY 2007. The second largest proposed decrease is the $28 million reduction for Land and Water Conservation Fund state grants. NPS is not authorized to use fee revenue to fund that program.

Question 2a. Maintenance Backlog: The construction portion of the budget has decreased by $84.5 million from the 2006 appropriation. This is the lowest amount requested for NPS construction projects in the past 5 years.

Will this decrease come solely from new construction project funds or will it also eliminate some maintenance projects required to reduce the backlog?

Answer. The 2007 budget request focuses on protecting and maintaining existing assets rather than funding new construction projects. Assuming the President's budget request is funded, NPS intends to sustain the progress made in the asset management program, as measured by the facility condition index.

Question 2b. By looking closely at project data sheets in the green books for FY06 and FY07, it appears that the majority of the cut in construction funding (over $74 million) is from major maintenance (see chart). Does this mean that the Administration has achieved the President's goal of fixing the maintenance backlog and is now shifting it's priorities to other areas?

Answer. The proposed $84.5 million reduction in construction will reduce the number of projects overall, but the majority of the reduction will be in new construction projects. According to the Department's classifications, of the $121.9 million requested for line-item construction, $39.3 million, or 32 percent, of the funding is for new construction. In 2006, $104.9 million, or 53 percent, of the line-item construction dollars were programmed for new park facilities. The Administration still considers addressing the NPS deferred maintenance backlog a priority. The FY 2007 budget request includes $933 million in deferred maintenance funding for FY 2007—an amount equal to the average annual amount of funding provided from FY 2002 to FY 2006, but distributed differently among the various facility-related accounts from previous years.

Question 2c. What type of long range program have you implemented to track the maintenance backlog and prioritize future maintenance requirements?

Answer. The NPS is transforming the agency's approach to managing its facilities. During the past four years, NPS has been implementing an asset management program focused on developing, for the first time, a comprehensive inventory and condition assessment of the agency's asset base. Parks have completed, for the first time, a prioritization of their asset inventory. Condition assessments on eight industry-standard assets (such as buildings, water systems, roads and trails) will be completed at all parks by the end of 2006. This shift in emphasis for the agency is based on management reforms and performance measures, and features a state-of-the-art software system. These new tools will allow NPS to have a better understanding of the true cost of ownership, including recurring operational costs of the facilities found in parks. Once condition assessments are completed, NPS will have a better understanding of the current deferred maintenance needs.

Question 3a. Grand Teton National Park Transportation Plan: Several years ago, Grand Teton National Park began a long term transportation planning process. We still do not have a plan completed.

What is causing the delay?

Answer. The Grand Teton transportation plan has taken a long time, but NPS is in the final stages of completing it. Part of the delay is attributable to restarting the plan in 2004 after a decision was made to focus on actions that are achievable within a 5-10 year period.

The draft plan was released for public comment in the summer of 2005, and the park is now analyzing and developing responses to the more than 2,600 comments it received. We anticipate releasing the final plan/EIS in the fall of 2006, and signing a record of decision in the winter of 2006/2007.

Question 3b. How much funding do you estimate it will take to complete the plan?

Answer. We estimate that it will cost $75,000 to complete the plan and related compliance. NPS has spent $684,000 on the plan since 2001 using a combination of park entrance fee revenue, NPS alternative transportation program funds, and Teton County funds.

Question 3c. Will this budget provide enough to finish the Teton transportation planning process?

Answer. We plan to use $75,000 in park entrance fee revenue, not appropriated funds, to complete the plan.

Question 4a. The proposed budget has placed funding for National Heritage Areas under the Historic Preservation Fund.

What authority do you have to fund National Heritage Areas in this manner?

Answer. We believe that the appropriation language submitted with the President's Fiscal Year 2007 budget request would provide sufficient authority to fund the National Heritage Area program under the Historic Preservation Fund.

Question 4b. Will the use of the Historic Preservation Fund for National Heritage Areas cause a reduction in funds for preservation grants and other funds provided to State Historic Preservation Offices?

Answer. No. The amount proposed in the FY 2007 request for preservation grants and other funds provided to State Historic Preservation Offices is not affected by the inclusion of funding for National Heritage Areas in the Historic Preservation Fund account.

Question 5. Visitor Services: The Administration proposes to offset a $1.6 million cut in visitor services with revenue from filming permits. This law has been in place for many years. Why do you anticipate an increase in revenue from this source in 2007?

Answer. We expect parks to have the ability to begin collecting fees for commercial filming and certain still photography well before the start of FY 2007. As a temporary measure, to expedite implementation of the NPS commercial filming law (P.L. 106-206), a rule will be published very shortly to revoke the portion of 43 CFR 5.1 that prohibits NPS from collecting fees for filming. Thirty days after that rule is published, if no significant negative comments are received, parks will have the ability to collect commercial filming fees based on the fee schedule currently being used by the Nevada office of the Bureau of Land Management and in accordance with procedures explained in a guidance memo from the Director.

As a long-term measure, the Department expects to publish this year a revised version of 43 CFR 5.1 that has been approved by the NPS, the U.S. Fish & Wildlife Service, and the Bureau of Land Management. That proposal will have a 60-day public comment period. It will be followed by publication of a proposed location fee schedule, which will also have a public comment period.

Question 6. Visitor Services: The Administration's budget projects a $6.5 million decrease in fixed costs for interpretation and education Rangers. Why are fixed costs for this program declining while fixed costs for other programs are increasing?

Answer. The $6.6 million reduction in the "fixed costs and related changes" column of the Interpretation and Education program in the NPS Budget Justifications reflects a shift of funding for one entity from one account to another. Funding for the Harpers Ferry Center ($10.4 million) was moved from Interpretation and Education to the Construction account, in order to place the NPS interpretive design center in the same account as the construction design center (Denver Service Center). Had the Harpers Ferry Center remained in Interpretation and Education, the funding for that program would have shown a $3.8 million increase for FY 2007.

Question 7a. Personal Watercraft: The NPS has been bogged down with a personal watercraft rulemaking for over six years.

What is the reason for the delays, and what, if any, additional resources would help get this process back on track and the rulemakings completed?

Answer. In 2000, when the NPS reached a settlement agreement with the Bluewater Network, the NPS committed to evaluating eight resource topics through the NEPA process for each affected park unit. The analyses to fully consider these topics were more involved than anticipated. While the NEPA analyses and promulgation of rules has taken a long time, at this point, rulemaking has been completed for all but five units. The status of those are as follows:

- The final rule for Gulf Islands National Seashore is currently under final signature review and should be published in the Federal Register in the very near future.
- The final rules for Cape Lookout National Seashore should be published before the summer season.
- The final rules for Gateway National Recreation Area and Curecanti National Recreation Area should be published during mid-summer of 2006.
- Big Thicket National Preserve is finishing its NEPA work.

Question 7b. Since the NPS has completed 15 of 15 favorable environmental assessments regarding the use of personal watercraft—Will the NPS consider revisiting this PWC rule system wide—Particularly to allow the use of PWCs in the parks that are still mired in the rulemaking process?

Answer. At this time, the NPS has no plans to revisit the use of PWCs system-wide. Determination for PWC use at any park is based on an assessment of a unit's legislative history, regulatory authorities, and analysis of sound, air quality, wildlife safety concerns, visitor use, and the purpose for the park as described in its authorizing legislation. Each determination is made with public participation, including public meetings and participation by advisory commissions and State and local governments. As noted above, we are close to finishing work on the five remaining park units where PWC rulemaking has not been completed.

RESPONSES OF FRAN MAINELLA TO QUESTIONS FROM SENATOR TALENT

Thank you for holding this hearing. I think it is important that we look in to the budget for the Park Service and I thank the witness for appearing before this committee.

Question 1. I am a supporter of Heritage Areas—and I am hoping to get heritage area designations in Missouri because I believe that they are a good way to bring interested parties under the umbrella of one advisory board to make decisions about a site or region. Please respond to the following questions regarding Heritage Areas and the impact on property rights.

Have the boundaries of heritage areas expanded after the original designation?

Answer. There have been at least two National Heritage Areas that have added counties to their boundaries at the request of the local coordinating entity who manages the area, based on public support, relationship to the themes of the heritage area, and action by Congress. Because a feasibility study is required to be completed prior to designation, the boundaries of a National Heritage Area are normally drawn to include all the appropriate resources that relate to the national story and do not need to be revised after designation.

Question 2. What percentage of heritage areas have non profits on their boards?

Answer. Of the 27 National Heritage Areas, 12 have non-profit organizations as the local coordinating entity that are responsible for preparing a management plan for the area and implementing the initiatives identified in the plan. One area, Hudson River Valley National Heritage Area, is ,jointly coordinated by a State agency and non-profit while another, the Ohio and Erie National Heritage Canalway, is coordinated by a Federal Commission that is. staffed by a non-profit corporation. In addition, several that are coordinated by Federal Commissions also have non-profit groups represented on their boards.

Question 3. What oversight does the park service have over the funding? Could that be written into legislation at the time of designation?

Answer. Generally, funds are appropriated through the National Park Service budget to the National Heritage Area. The NPS develops a cooperative agreement to provide the funding to the National Heritage Area and to provide oversight on how the funds are spent. Each area is required to hire an independent auditor who provides the NPS with an annual audit relating to Federal expenditures by the local coordinating entity.

National Heritage Areas program legislation, currently pending in Congress, would also require each area to prepare an annual report to be submitted to the Secretary for each fiscal year that Federal funds are received. This report would specify performance goals and accomplishments, expenditures, grants made to other entities, amounts and sources of matching funds, and other funds leveraged by Federal dollars.

Question 4. Does a heritage designation limit landowners access to their private lands?

Answer. No. Designation as a National Heritage Area places no restrictions on the use, development, or access of private lands located within the area's boundary. In addition, authorizing legislation for all recently designated National Heritage Areas protects private property owners by specifically forbidding public access to private property without owner consent.

Question 5. Missourians have shared with me three specific instances where heritage areas have resulted in infringements on property rights—inverse condemnation of property owned by individuals for the Appalachian Trail in Virginia; efforts in theBuffalo National River area to eliminate 1,000-1,100 homes; and efforts to purchase`land in the Cuyahoga Valley near Akron, Ohio. Please comment on these situations and their relationships to heritage areas.

Answer. The Appalachian National Scenic Trail, the Buffalo National River, and Cuyahoga Valley National Park are units of the National Park System, not National Heritage Areas. Each one has individual authority from Congress to acquire property under specified terms. The NPS has followed Congress' direction in both authorizing legislation and appropriations in acquiring property for those units. National Heritage Areas do not have Federal land acquisition authority except in rare cases where Congress has provided such authority.

National Heritage Area designation places no restrictions on owners of private property including zoning and land use regulations. The legislation for each designated area provides protection for private property rights tailored to the specific needs of the region.

Question 6. Do heritage areas pose a threat to private property rights in the area?

Answer. No. National Heritage Area designation places no restrictions on owners of private property including zoning and `land use regulations. All recently established National Heritage Areas have language in their authorizing legislation that explicitly protects the rights of private property owners. National Heritage Areas are based on the principle of collaborative conservation and have no regulatory elements. It should be noted that almost 49 million people live in the 27 designated National Heritage Areas. To date, we have found no examples of private property complaints stemming from a heritage area designation. A 2004 GAO report on National Heritage Areas concluded that the designation of a site as a National Heritage Area does not appear to directly affect the rights of private property owners.

Question 7. Does the advisory board, created by a heritage area have any authority over city, county, or state governments?

Answer. No. For each National Heritage Area designated by Congress, the authorizing legislation identifies the local coordinating entity that will be responsible for preparing a management plan for the area and implementing the initiatives identified in the plan. Participation in any project or activity associated with the National Heritage Area is voluntary. These management plans are developed with extensive public involvement including coordination with city, county and State governments. The establishment of a coordinating entity for the National Heritage Area does not impact any existing authorities held by any unit of state or local government; in fact, all recently established National Heritage Areas include language in their authorizing legislation stating this.

Question 8. Does the advisory board created by a heritage area have any authority over decisions made by a property owner?

Answer. No. The local coordinating entity has no authority over property owners on how they use their land, nor does it impose any additional burdens on any property owner. All recently established National Heritage Areas have included language in their authorizing legislation that explicitly protects the rights of private property owners.

Question 9. Does a heritage area lead to additional land purchases by the federal government?

Answer. The designation of a National Heritage Area is not meant to lead to land purchases by the Federal Government and in fact, most recently established National Heritage Areas have included language in their authorizing legislation that explicitly bar the local coordinating entity from using appropriated Federal dollars for acquiring real property or any interest in real property. Designation as a National Heritage Area does not affect who owns the land within the area. If it is privately owned before designation, then it privately owned after designation; the same applies to publicly owned land.

RESPONSES OF FRAN MAINELLA TO QUESTIONS FROM SENATOR SALAZAR

LAND AND WATER CONSERVATION FUND (LWCF)

Question 1. Director Mainella, the National Park Service recently published its 2005 State Land and Water Conservation Fund Annual Report, in which it concludes that the LWCF stateside grants program delivers excellent results. Your report says: "nearly 55 million visits at 44 state parks represents only a small sampling of visitor use at the estimated 40, 000 state and local park sites assisted by the program. Year in and year out, the Land and Water Conservation Fund works in partnership with states and communities to deliver and protect opportunities for outdoor recreation." Does the National Park Service stand by this endorsement of the LWCF stateside grants program?

Answer. Yes, the NPS stands by the statements in the report quoted above. For over four decades, NPS and its predecessor agencies have partnered with States and local units of government to provide public recreation opportunities through the 40,000 matching grants awarded through this program.

Question 2. Given the Park Service's own assessment of the efficiency and effectiveness of the LWCF stateside grant program can you explain why it is being eliminated in this year's budget?

Answer. The FY 2007 budget request does not include funding for Land and Water Conservation Fund State grants. As the Administration strives to trim the Federal deficit, focusing on core Federal agency responsibilities is imperative. Many of these grants support State and local parks that have alternative sources of funding through State revenues or bonds. In addition, a 2003 PART review found the current program could not adequately measure performance or demonstrate results. While the report you referenced includes some worthwhile information as to how the grants were used, the Administration remains committed to utilizing performance measures consistent with the Government Performance and Results Act.

Question 3. Has the National Park Service evaluated the effects that cutting the LWCF stateside grants program will have on projects currently being built in rural communities?

Answer. Regardless of where it is located, any project currently approved and being built should be completed. A project is not approved for a grant by NPS unless there are sufficient Federal funds in the grant award and an adequate local match to complete the project.

Question 4. How many of LWCF stateside projects are currently underway in rural communities?

Answer. There are currently 1,900 projects that have been approved but not yet completed throughout the nation. We have not determined how many of those are located in rural areas.

Question 5. How do you propose finding funding to complete them, if the stateside grants program is eliminated?

Answer. A project is not approved for a grant by NPS unless there are sufficient Federal funds in the grant award and an adequate local match to complete the project.

MAINTENANCE BACKLOG

Question 1. In 2000, the President promised to provide enough funding over five years to eliminate Park Service's maintenance backlog, which was estimated at the time to be $4.9 billion. It is now five years since that commitment and I am hearing estimates that place the NPS maintenance backlog somewhere between $4.5 billion to $9.69 billion. That is to say that the maintenance backlog at the Parks seems to have increased over the past five years. Is that right?

Answer. The estimated $4.9 billion maintenance backlog figure was identified in a 1998 General Accounting Office report ("Efforts to Identify and Manage the Maintenance Backlog" GAO/RCED-98-143). That figure represented a compilation of desired projects in parks that had not been validated by systematic, comprehensive assessments of the true asset conditions or prioritized by NPS.

We now know that the deferred maintenance backlog cannot be stated as a single, static dollar figure. What is important is the improved condition over time and knowing that the dollars spent made a difference in improving the condition of the asset. Our approach is to focus on what it will take to bring our assets to acceptable condition as measured by the facility condition index. For this reason, NPS is transforming the agency's approach to managing its facilities. Parks have completed, for the first time, a comprehensive inventory and prioritization of its asset base. NPS is also on track to complete comprehensive condition assessments on eight industry-standard assets (such as buildings, water systems, roads, and trails) by the end of 2006. Once these condition assessments are completed, NPS will have a better understanding of its current deferred maintenance needs. Our goal is to bring the portfolio of assets up to acceptable condition, with performance measures used to prioritize investments.

Question 2. What is the Department of the Interior's most recent estimate of the maintenance backlog at the Parks?

Answer. Please see the answer above.

Question 3. Do you have any projections of how the proposed budget for the National Parks will affect the total maintenance backlog, considering it will cut the construction and maintenance budget by $84.6 million, 27 percent?

Answer. The Administration remains committed to reducing the maintenance backlog within the National Park Service, and the NPS continues to make significant progress in completing the numerous projects necessary to improve the condition of park infrastructure. Since 2002, nearly 6,000 projects have been undertaken and approximately $4.7 billion have been invested using line-item construction, repair and rehabilitation, fee, and Federal Lands Highway dollars. The 2007 budget proposes to protect the Administration's past investments by realigning funding within the NPS asset management program to focus on proactive measures that will preclude these resources from slipping to poor condition.

The Cyclic Maintenance Program incorporates a number of regularly scheduled preventive maintenance procedures and preservation techniques into a comprehensive program that prolongs the life of a particular asset. The proposed increase in cyclic project funding would assist in preventing the continued deterioration of NPS assets. Increasing the project funding will afford parks the ability to maintain assets on a predictive cycle, rather than allowing them to fall into disrepair and ultimately adding to the backlog. Funds appropriated for the cyclic maintenance program would target those assets that are mission critical and still in maintainable condition, but could fall into poor condition without the proper application of life cycle maintenance. With the proposed increase of $10.0 million, the cyclic maintenance program now totals $71.5 million.

The 2007 budget includes $86.2 million for the Repair and Rehabilitation program. Over the past five years, $345 million has been allocated for this program. In 2007, NPS will continue to prioritize projects that address critical health and safety, resource protection, compliance, deferred maintenance, and minor capital improvement issues. The budget request also includes a proposal to use additional recreation fee revenue for facility maintenance projects. For 2007, the Department estimates that $100 million in recreation fees will be used for deferred maintenance projects.

Within the total proposed for construction, line-item construction projects are funded at $121.9 million. The budget request focuses on protecting and maintaining existing assets rather than funding new construction projects. Assuming the President's budget request is funded, NPS intends to sustain the progress made in the asset management program, as measured by the facility condition index.

REVISIONS TO PARK SERVICE POLICIES

Question 1. I and many of my colleagues have repeatedly expressed our opposition to the proposed changes to the National Park Service's policies. We feel that they undermine the core mission of the Park Service and are, quite frankly, unnecessary. Visitor satisfaction at our parks, after all, is over 95%, and the public seems quite satisfied with the existing policies, which were updated just five years ago. I appreciate you agreeing to extend your consideration of the policy changes another six months, but I do wonder how much this whole exercise is costing the taxpayer. What has been the cost—to date—in staff time, resources, etc., of your efforts to revise the current management policies?

Answer. Periodic review and development of all types of management and policy documents are included within the duties of NPS employees and are not calculated separately.

The NPS has a special web site programmed to efficiently process the large volume of comments they sometimes receive on documents that are released for public review. A contractor has been retained at a cost of approximately $39,000 to help sort and organize the Management Policies comments that have been submitted through this web site.

Question 2. What do you expect the cost to be over the next year if you continue to consider revising these policies?

Answer. The only additional expense associated with this effort that we currently anticipate is the cost of printing the revised policies. At this time, we do not have an estimate of that cost.

Question 3. Considering that these policies were revised just five years ago, and given all the other needs in the Parks, is this really the best use of the Park Service's energy and resources at this time?

Answer. We believe that revised and improved policies are needed because managers face continuing challenges as we preserve the parks while striving to serve our visitors and partner with our local communities. Every day, without fail, we are tested when we make decisions on what to do or what not to do; what to build or what not to build; what to allow or what not to allow. From these challenges, we learn and improve our practices.

NATIONAL HERITAGE AREAS

Question 1. According to the National Park Service, National Heritage Areas "preserve and celebrate many of America's defining landscapes." I find this to be true in Colorado—the Cache La Poudre NHA empowers local communities to work collaboratively with the state and federal governments to craft solutions that protect their natural landscape. The program is so effective in spurring collaborative conservation that I, with the support of the local communities, have introduced legislation to designate the South Park National Heritage Area and the Sangre de Cristo National Heritage Area in Colorado. These are two crown jewels of the American landscape and are worthy of NHA protection.

Many of the existing national heritage areas are in their early phases and need Park Service expertise and support to get on their feet. If the Administration is in fact committed to supporting collaborative conservation, why is the Administration cutting funding for these great partnerships?

Answer. The Administration is committed to supporting National Heritage Areas. The Administration's request for FY 2007 for Heritage Partnership Programs is $2.374 million more than the Administration's request for FY 2006. The Heritage Partnership Programs are a critical component of the Department's new umbrella activity, America's Heritage and Preservation Partnership Program, which will also include Save America's Treasures and Preserve America. Even after Federal funding for a National Heritage Area reaches its authorized limit, the NPS continues to provide technical support to the area indefinitely.

Question 2. I also find it puzzling that the Administration is proposing to shift funding for this program from National Recreation and Preservation and into the Historic Preservation Fund. In the West, our heritage areas are about far more than historic resources. They are about protecting the land, culture, and resources that underpin our way of life. Do you agree that heritage areas are about protecting more than the historic resources of a place?

Answer. Yes, we agree that National Heritage Areas are about preserving natural, cultural, scenic, and recreational resources as well as historic resources.

Question 3. Why, then, is the funding being shifted to Historic Preservation?

Answer. Funding for National Heritage Areas is being shifted to the Historic Preservation Fund as part of the America's Heritage and Preservation Partnership Program, which also encompasses two Historic Preservation Fund grants programs

(Save America's Treasures and Preserve America). The combination of these three programs represents a more seamless approach to supporting locally focused historic preservation and heritage tourism programs that will allow local communities to determine which strategies best suit their heritage needs; apply to the most appropriate programs to conserve heritage resources and promote heritage tourism; and better and more efficiently coordinate cultural resource preservation.

Question 4. Does this shift in funding sources imply that the National Park Service is changing the mission of national heritage areas so that they focus primarily on historic resources?

Answer. No, the mission of the Heritage Partnership Programs remains the same, to preserve nationally important natural, cultural, historic, scenic and recreational resources through locally driven partnership efforts.

RESPONSES OF FRAN MAINELLA TO QUESTIONS FROM SENATOR MENENDEZ

Question 1. Could you explain why the Management Policies needed to be rewritten?

Answer. At an April 25, 2002, hearing called by the House Subcommittee on National Parks, Recreation, and Public Lands, Congressman Radanovich, who was then chairman of the subcommittee, requested that Director Mainella initiate a comprehensive review of the 2001 edition of Management Policies. Among other things, the chairman perceived that the policies did not adequately reflect the Service's responsibilities under the 1916 Organic Act to provide for enjoyment of the parks. Chairman Radanovich again inquired about a review in a June 6, 2002, letter to the Director. In a September 24, 2003 letter to Chairman Radanovich, the Director stated that the NPS had begun a systematic review.

In response to this continuing congressional interest, and since management of the national park system is always a matter of general concern to the Department of the Interior, a Departmental goal was adopted to "Improve the NPS Management Policies." Deputy Assistant Secretary Paul Hoffman, who provides policy guidance to the NPS, was tasked with lead responsibility on behalf of the Department. In July 2005, Mr. Hoffman presented for the NPS's review his initial recommendations for updates to the policies. This was an internal document intended only to be a starting point for discussion.

At a December 14, 2005, House Subcommittee hearing on the NPS Organic Act, Congressman Pearce, the new chairman of the subcommittee, acknowledged the controversy over the Management Policies review. He reaffirmed that "it was this subcommittee in April 2002—not Deputy Assistant Secretary Paul Hoffman—that initiated an evaluation of the 2001 NPS Management Policies . . . ." Upon receiving Deputy Assistant Secretary Hoffman's preliminary rough draft, the Director assigned NPS career employees to review and evaluate the suggestions. The suggestions were to be considered along with other NPS policy initiatives that would improve the 2001 Management Policies. For example, the Service already had an acknowledged need to: place more emphasis on civic engagement and public involvement; update the planning procedures in Chapter 2; correct some aspects of the wilderness stewardship procedures in Chapter 6; and discourage construction projects that are excessive in size or cost, or too expensive to operate. Also, this was an opportunity to also address any new laws, executive orders, and regulations that had not already been addressed in the 2001 edition.

Several other factors came into play in seeing this as a positive opportunity for the NPS. For example, the update would take into account: the NPS's increased responsibilities for protecting our borders and icon parks against terrorists; changes in the demographics of visitors; rapid population growth around parks; improvements in technology that provide new ways to enjoy parks or reduce adverse impacts on resources; and a new focus on cooperative conservation.

Question 2. Could you describe the latest situation with Ellis Island, and why it has taken so long to approve a plan for the site?

Answer. At the urging of Congress, the NPS and the Department over that past few years have applied a great deal of oversight to the type of partnership projects called for in the Ellis Island plan. This review and consultation is necessary to assure that realistic and achievable expectations result from NPS planning documents and partnership agreements. NPS is making final revisions to the Development Concept Plan/Draft Environmental Impact Statement for Ellis Island and is preparing to integrate the plan's concepts into the Partnership Construction Process.

Question 3. Under the draft Management Policies, would the Park Service allow off-road vehicle use at the Delaware Water Gap National Recreation Area? Would it be considered an "appropriate use?" What guidelines would regulate the use of vehicles around the park? How would we measure the impact on the park's guests, the wildlife, and the preservation mandate of the NPS? What steps would be taken to maintain a balance between off-road vehicle use and other forms of park recreation?

Answer. The draft Management Policies would not change the process by which off-road vehicle (ORV) use is determined or regulated at Delaware Water Gap National Recreation Area or at any other unit of the National Park System. The draft policies are clear that ORV use in national park units is governed by the same Executive Orders and regulations that govern ORV use currently. The proposed change for the section on ORV use in the draft policies is new wording that is simpler and less negative in tone. And, the draft policies are subject to further change as we go through the revision process.

ORV use is not allowed at Delaware Water Gap NRA at present. Under the draft policies, as under the current Management Policies, a special regulation would have to be promulgated for that purpose. Among other things, developing a special regulation would require a full environmental analysis under the National Environmental Policy Act, which would include public review of the process.

○

CPSIA information can be obtained
at www.ICGtesting.com
Printed in the USA
BVHW04s1040210918
528173BV00023B/1958/P

9 781527 960152